Easy and Safe Stretching to Do After Age 60 Explained Step-by-Step

(To Improve Posture, To Alleviate Back Pain, and To Prevent Injuries)

Chase Williams

Table of Contents

Chapter 1: Introduction: Why Stretching is Essential After 60 • An overview of the importance of stretching in later life.

Chapter 2: Understanding Your Body at 60 and Beyond • A guide on how your body changes with age and what that means for your exercise routine.

Chapter 3: Basic Principles of Stretching • Fundamentals and techniques of stretching to get you started on the right foot.

Chapter 4: Preparing for Stretching • Tips on warming up and preparation to prevent injuries.

Chapter 5: Stretching for Perfect Posture
• Targeted exercises for improving posture.

Chapter 6: Easing Tension: Stretching for Back Pain
• Focused approaches for the best stretching techniques to relieve back pain.

Chapter 7: Stretching for Legs and Knees
• Specific exercises to maintain leg health and prevent common issues.

Chapter 8: Extend Your Reach: Stretching for Shoulders and Neck
• Strategies to ease tension in the shoulders and neck.

Chapter 9: Flexibility for Hands and Wrists

- Stretching specifically aimed at keeping hands and wrists agile.

Chapter 10: Breathing Exercises and Stretching
- How breathing can properly boost your stretching routine.

Chapter 11: Preventing Injuries: What to Avoid
- Tips on how to stretch safely to avoid injuries.

Chapter 12: Daily Stretching Routine
- A daily action plan for maintaining bodily flexibility.

Chapter 13: Stretching for Specific Activities
- How to adjust your stretching routine for activities such as gardening, golfing, and walking.

Chapter 14: Seasonality and Stretching
• How to adapt your stretching routine to different seasons.

Chapter 15: Stretching and Nutrition
• How diet can lessen or enhance the effectiveness of stretching exercises.

Chapter 16: Stretching for Cardiovascular Health

• The impact of stretching on circulation and heart health.

Chapter 17: The Importance of Rest and Recovery
• Relaxing stretches to improve sleep and muscle recovery.

Chapter 18: Stretching for Mental Health

- How stretching can aid in managing stress and anxiety.

Chapter 19: Stretching in Water
- Techniques and benefits of stretching in pools or the sea.

Chapter 20: Stretching and Balance
- Exercises to improve balance and prevent falls.

Chapter 21: Apparel and Equipment for Stretching
- Guidelines for the best choices for effective and comfortable workouts.

Chapter 22: Stretching and Joint Mobility
- Focusing on joint health through targeted exercises.

Chapter 23: Stretching for Active Aging
• Tips for incorporating stretching into an active lifestyle.

Chapter 24: Travel and Stretching
• How to maintain a stretching routine while traveling.

Chapter 25: Community and Stretching
• How to involve friends and family in your stretching routine for collective commitment.

Chapter 26: FAQs - Frequently Asked Questions on Stretching and the Elderly
• Answers to common questions and misconceptions.

Chapter 27: Conclusion and Action Plan
• A summary and recommendations on how to implement a daily stretching routine.

Introduction

Dear Readers,

Have you ever wondered why some people seem to age more gracefully than others? Why some individuals in their seventies are more energetic and vibrant than those much younger? The secret might be simpler than you think, and it's literally within reach—or rather, within your body.

Welcome to the book that could forever change how you see and live your "golden years." In these pages, you'll discover a treasure trove of easy and safe stretching exercises, designed specifically for people like you: individuals who want to live life to the fullest without letting age become a hindrance.

Imagine waking up every morning without that nagging back pain that's been haunting you for years. Imagine being able to play with your grandchildren, to walk, run, or even dance as if time hasn't left its mark. This is not a dream; it's an attainable goal, and the key is stretching.

Stretching is more than just a morning routine or a practice reserved for athletes. It's a life philosophy, an investment in your future, and a form of self-care. And the good news is, it's never too late to start.

In "Easy and Safe Stretching Techniques for Those Over 60: Step-By-Step Guide to Better Posture, Back Pain Relief, and Injury Prevention," I will guide you through a series of exercises that you can easily integrate into your daily life. Step by step, I will show you how to improve your posture, relieve back pain, and prevent injuries that could limit your mobility.

This book is your manual for a healthier, more active, and happier life. Each chapter is a milestone in your journey toward well-being, and I am thrilled to be a part of it. Don't waste any more time; let's begin this journey together.

Wishing you an enlightening read and a future in perfect shape.

with affection and optimism,
Chase Williams

About the Author: Chase Williams Chase Williams is not your typical fitness guru. Born and raised in a small Midwest town, Chase initially embarked on a career in engineering. However, life had other plans for him. After facing a debilitating injury that put him out of commission for months, Chase realized the importance of physical well-being as he went through his own rehabilitation process. This life-altering experience ignited a new passion in him: to make wellness and fitness accessible for everyone, regardless of age or physical condition. Chase returned to school, this time to study kinesiology and exercise science. Specializing in geriatric exercise, he earned his certification as a personal trainer with a focus on elderly clients. He has spent the last decade working with senior citizens, helping them regain their mobility, improve their posture, and enjoy a healthier, more active lifestyle. His first book, "Easy and Safe Stretching Techniques for Those Over 60: Step-By-Step Guide to Better Posture, Back Pain Relief, and Injury Prevention," is a culmination of his years of experience and research. Combining science-backed techniques with heartwarming personal anecdotes, Chase's writing style is both informative and engaging. He knows how to break down complex concepts into easily understandable terms, making the book a valuable resource for its target audience. Chase is not just an author and a personal trainer; he's also an advocate for change in how society views aging and physical fitness. He regularly speaks at wellness seminars, volunteers at senior centers, and collaborates with healthcare professionals to promote the importance of an active lifestyle in the golden years. When not writing or training clients, Chase enjoys hiking, amateur photography, and spending quality time with his family. He currently resides in Boulder, Colorado, where he runs his own fitness studio tailored specifically to older adults.

Chapter 1: Introduction - Why Stretching is Essential After 60

Welcome to the first chapter of this journey towards a healthier and more active life. If you've chosen to read this book, it's because you've grasped a fundamental truth: well-being has no age limit. And in these pages, you will find the tools to make this statement a concrete reality in your daily life.

Aging and the Human Body

Aging is a natural process that we all face. As time passes, it's inevitable to notice changes in the structure and functions of our body. Tendons and ligaments become less elastic, joint mobility decreases, and muscular strength tends to decline. That's why, especially after the age of 60, it becomes crucial to maintain an exercise regimen that takes these changes into account.

The Importance of Stretching

Stretching is much more than a random series of movements. It's a practice aimed at improving your quality of life on multiple fronts: increasing flexibility, reducing the risk of injury, and enhancing overall health. A good stretching routine can also help to alleviate muscle pain and improve posture, two aspects that often become problematic as we age.

A Book for Everyone

This book is not just for those who already engage in regular physical activity. It's a manual that serves everyone, regardless of their fitness level. The exercises suggested have been carefully chosen and described in such a way that they can be easily performed by anyone, safely.

What You Will Find in This Book

In the subsequent chapters, we'll explore a variety of specific exercises, each with detailed instructions and tips on how to perform them in the most effective and safe manner possible. From stretching for posture to exercises that relieve back pain, to techniques for injury prevention, this book is your ideal companion for a healthier and more active life after 60.

With these goals in mind, we invite you to continue reading, armed with open-mindedness and determination. Because, as an ancient proverb says, "You're never too old to learn."

Happy reading and happy journey towards well-being!

Chapter 2: Understanding Your Body at 60 and Beyond

As we age, our body undergoes changes that can impact how we feel, move, and generally live. This chapter is dedicated to exploring how the body changes after 60 and how these changes can affect your exercise routine and overall well-being.

Section 1: Physiological Changes and What They Mean for You

- **Loss of Muscle Mass**: A reduction in muscle mass is a normal feature of aging. This means maintaining or increasing muscle mass through resistance exercises may become a priority.
- **Decreased Elasticity and Flexibility**: Ligaments and tendons become less elastic, making it harder to perform certain movements and increasing the risk of injuries. Stretching and yoga exercises can be particularly helpful.
- **Decreased Bone Density**: As we age, bone density may decline, increasing the risk of fractures. Weight-bearing exercises like walking and light

jogging can help maintain bone health.

Section 2: The Impact of Hormones

- **Testosterone**: The production of testosterone decreases with age, which can affect muscle mass and energy levels.
- **Thyroid Hormones**: A decline in thyroid hormone production can slow metabolism, making weight management more challenging.

Section 3: Nutrition and Supplementation

- **Calcium and Vitamin D**: For bone health, adequate intake of calcium and Vitamin D is essential. Consult a doctor before starting any supplementation program.

- **Protein**: Adequate protein intake is crucial for maintaining muscle mass.

Section 4: Practical Tips for Exercise Routine

- **Low-Impact Exercises**: Sports like swimming or walking are easy on the joints and can be easily incorporated into your daily routine.
- **Stretching and Flexibility**: A stretching program can improve mobility and reduce pain and the risk of injuries.

Section 5: Consulting Health Professionals

Before starting or modifying any exercise routine, it's always a good idea to consult your physician, especially if you have preexisting health conditions such as heart issues, diabetes, or hypertension.

With this guide to understanding your body at 60 and beyond, we hope you feel more prepared and informed in making healthy choices that will allow you to enjoy a high quality of life for the years to come.

Chapter 3: Fundamentals of Stretching

Stretching is a key component of any exercise routine, especially as we age. This chapter explores the basics and techniques of stretching, also providing detailed exercise examples to get you started on the right foot.

Section 1: Why Stretching is Important

- **Improves Flexibility**: Regular stretching can improve flexibility, which is essential for overall mobility.
- **Reduces Risk of Injuries**: A more flexible muscle is less likely to incur injuries such as strains or tears.
- **Improves Circulation**: Stretching can help improve blood flow, which is beneficial for heart health and can also speed up muscle recovery.

Section 2: Types of Stretching

1. **Static**: This involves stretching a muscle and holding it in a fixed position for a certain amount of time.

2. **Dynamic**: This type of stretching involves movements that stretch muscles to their maximum extent, but without holding the position.

Section 3: General Rules

- **Warm-up**: It's always good practice to perform a brief warm-up before stretching to prepare the muscles.
- **Don't Overdo It**: Stretching should never cause pain. If you feel pain, it means you're pushing too hard.
- **Duration**: For static stretching, each position should be held for at least 15-30 seconds.

Section 4: Stretching Exercise Examples

- **Quadricep Stretch**
    1. Stand up, grab your right foot with your right hand

and pull it towards your glutes.
2. Hold the position for 20-30 seconds.
3. Repeat for the other side.

- **Hamstring Stretch**
  1. Sit with one leg extended and the other bent so that the foot touches the thigh of the extended leg.
  2. Bend forward at the waist, trying to touch the toe of the extended leg.
  3. Hold for 20-30 seconds and then switch legs.
- **Calf Stretch**
  1. Stand close to a wall, put your hands against the wall.
  2. Put one foot behind the other and slightly bend the front knee, keeping the

back knee straight and the heel on the ground.
3. Hold the position for 20-30 seconds and then switch sides.

By following these principles and examples, you'll be well-equipped to start an effective and safe stretching routine tailored to your needs.

Chapter 4: Getting Ready for Stretching

Before diving into stretching exercises, it's crucial to take time to prepare and warm up to prevent injuries and maximize benefits. This chapter offers an in-depth guide on how to prepare effectively.

Section 1: The Importance of Warming Up

- Increase in muscle temperature: A good warm-up increases muscle temperature, making them more elastic and less prone to injuries.
- Improved circulation: Warming up helps to improve blood circulation, providing essential oxygen and nutrients to muscles that are about to be exercised.

Section 2: Types of Warm-ups

1. Cardio Warm-up: A brief period of cardiovascular exercise, such as walking or cycling, is useful to increase the heart rate.
2. Dynamic Warm-up: Movements like joint rotations or light dynamic stretching exercises prepare the specific muscles that will be used during the stretching session.

Section 3: Duration and Intensity

- Duration: An effective warm-up should last at least 5-10 minutes.
- Intensity: The intensity should be moderate, sufficient to raise the heart rate but not so intense as to cause fatigue.

Section 4: Warm-up Exercise Examples

- Fast Walking
    1. Walk at a brisk pace for at least 5 minutes.
    2. Focus on deep breathing, inhaling and exhaling completely.
- Shoulder Rotations
    1. Standing, slowly rotate the shoulders forward for 10 repetitions.

2. Rotate the shoulders backward for another 10 repetitions.
- Wrist Rotations
    1. Extend your arms in front of you.
    2. Slowly rotate your wrists clockwise for 10 repetitions and then counter-clockwise for another 10 repetitions.
- Knee Raises
    1. Standing, raise your right knee as high as possible towards the chest.
    2. Hold for a few seconds and then lower slowly.
    3. Repeat for the left side and continue for 10 repetitions on each side.

By following these guidelines and exercises, you will be well-prepared for an effective and safe stretching session, minimizing the risk of injuries and maximizing the benefits for your flexibility and overall well-being.

Chapter 5: Stretching for Perfect Posture

Posture is a fundamental aspect of our overall health that we often neglect. Proper posture not only helps prevent pain and tension but also contributes to a more confident appearance and better breathing. This chapter is dedicated to specific stretching exercises to improve your posture.

Section 1: The Importance of Good Posture

- Spinal health: Good posture supports the health of the

spine, reducing pressure on discs and spinal nerves.
- Improved breathing: Maintaining good posture opens up the airways, thereby improving breathing and oxygenation of the body.

Section 2: Common Causes of Poor Posture

1. Sedentary lifestyle: A sedentary lifestyle can lead to weak muscles that do not adequately support the spine.
2. Excessive use of electronic devices: Looking down at phones or tablets for extended periods can cause poor posture.

Section 3: Basic Principles for Good Posture

- Alignment: Focus on aligning your head, shoulders, and hips.

- Balance: Maintain a balanced body weight on both feet.

Section 4: Examples of Stretching Exercises for Posture

- Neck and Shoulder Stretch
    1. Sitting or standing, tilt your head to one side, trying to touch your ear to your shoulder.
    2. Hold for 15-20 seconds.
    3. Repeat on the other side.
- Thoracic Rotations
    1. Sitting in a chair, with your feet planted on the ground, place your hands behind your head.
    2. Rotate your torso to the left, trying to look over your left shoulder.
    3. Hold for 15-20 seconds and repeat on the right side.
- Spine Extension

1. Standing, place your hands on your hips.
2. Stretch backward, pushing your hips forward and retracting your shoulders.
3. Hold for 15-20 seconds.

- Hip Flexor Stretch
    1. Kneeling on a mat, take a step forward with your right foot and bend your knee at 90 degrees.
    2. Slightly push your hips forward, keeping your upper body upright.
    3. Hold for 20-30 seconds and then switch sides.

By following these examples and principles, you will be on your way to improving your posture, preventing issues that can arise from improper posture. Remember, the key is consistency and commitment in keeping these exercises as part of your daily routine.

Chapter 6: Easing the Tension: Stretching for Back Pain

Introduction

Back pain is one of the most common ailments in people over the age of 60. Often, the pain is the result of years of poor posture, physical exertion, and the inevitable aging process. However, there's good news: with a series of targeted stretching exercises, you can ease tension and significantly improve your quality of life. In this chapter, we will explore some of the best stretching techniques to alleviate back pain.

Sub-chapter: Factors Contributing to Back Pain

Before diving into specific exercises, it's important to understand the factors that can contribute to back pain, such as weakened muscles, poor posture, and pre-existing conditions.

Exercise 1: Seated Forward Bend

1. Sit in a chair with a straight back and feet flat on the ground.
2. Lean forward from your waist, trying to reach your toes with your hands.
3. Hold the position for 15-20 seconds.
4. Slowly return to the starting position.

Benefits: This exercise helps to stretch the back muscles and improve spine flexibility.

Exercise 2: Trunk Rotation

1. Sit in a chair, keeping your back straight.
2. Place your right hand on your left leg and your left hand behind you on the chair.
3. Rotate your torso to the left and try to look over your left shoulder.
4. Hold for 15-20 seconds.
5. Repeat on the other side.

Benefits: This exercise stretches the oblique muscles and relieves tension in the lower back.

Exercise 3: Cat-Cow

1. Get on all fours on the mat, with hands under your shoulders and knees under your hips.
2. Inhale as you arch your back downward, pushing your pelvis and head upward (Cow position).
3. Exhale as you round your back upward, bringing your chin toward your chest (Cat position).
4. Perform 10-15 repetitions.

Benefits: This exercise is excellent for spine mobility and stretching back muscles.

Exercise 4: Back Extension

1. Lie face down on a mat or soft surface.
2. Place your hands on the ground at shoulder level.

3. Gently push with your hands, slowly lifting your torso and arching your back in extension. Make sure to keep your hips on the ground.
4. Hold the position for 15-20 seconds, then slowly return to the starting position.
5. Repeat 3-5 times.

Benefits: Stretches the front torso muscles and strengthens the paraspinal muscles of the back.

Exercise 5: Psoas Stretch

1. Start in a lunge position with your right foot forward.
2. Bend your right knee to 90 degrees and shift your weight forward until you feel a stretch in the front of your left hip.

3. Raise your arms upward and slightly lean back to increase the stretch.
4. Hold for 20-30 seconds, then switch sides.

Benefits: The psoas muscle can contribute to back pain when it's shortened. This exercise helps to lengthen it, potentially alleviating pain.

Exercise 6: Lateral Tilt

1. Stand with your feet shoulder-width apart.
2. Keeping your hands along your sides, slowly lean to the right, trying to slide your right hand down your leg.
3. Hold the stretch for 15-20 seconds, feeling a stretch along the left side of your body.
4. Return to the center and repeat on the other side.

Benefits: Stretches the oblique and intercostal muscles, offering relief from lateral back tension.

Always remember to perform exercises with slow and controlled movements, avoiding abrupt movements or those that cause pain. If an exercise causes pain or discomfort, discontinue it immediately and consult a doctor or physiotherapist.

Conclusion

Regular stretching can work wonders for back pain. It's important to remember, however, that if pain persists or worsens, it's crucial to consult a doctor for an accurate diagnosis and a personalized treatment plan.

Note: This information does not replace professional medical advice. It's always best to consult a doctor or physiotherapist before starting any new exercise routine.

***Chapter* 7**: Stretching for Legs and Knees Introduction Legs are the foundation of our body, allowing us to walk, run, jump, and perform a myriad of other physical activities. However, as we age, our leg muscles can weaken and become more susceptible to injuries and fatigue. This chapter is dedicated to targeted stretching exercises to keep legs and knees in good shape and prevent common issues like joint pain and muscle cramps.

Exercise 1: Quadriceps Stretch

1. Stand next to a wall or chair for balance.
2. Grab one foot with the corresponding hand, bending the knee.
3. Hold the position for 20-30 seconds, feeling a stretch in the front of the thigh.
4. Switch sides and repeat. Benefits: This exercise is excellent for stretching the quadriceps, the front muscles of the thighs, which are crucial for walking and standing up from a chair.

Exercise 2: Hamstring Stretch

1. Sit on a chair with your feet planted on the ground.
2. Extend one leg forward, keeping the heel on the ground and toes pointing upward.

3. Lean forward at the waist, trying to reach your foot with your hands.
4. Hold the position for 20-30 seconds and then switch legs. Benefits: Effectively stretches the hamstrings, the back muscles of the thighs, helps improve flexibility, and reduces lower back tension.

Exercise 3: Calf Stretch

1. Stand about a meter away from a wall.
2. Step one foot back, slightly bending the front knee.
3. Keep both heels on the ground and push your hips forward.
4. Hold the position for 20-30 seconds, then switch sides. Benefits: This exercise stretches the calf muscles, which are often under tension, especially

if you wear high heels or walk on uneven terrain.

Exercise 4: Ankle Rotations

1. Sit on a chair with your legs extended.
2. Lift one foot and start rotating the ankle clockwise for 10 times.
3. Change direction, rotating counterclockwise for another 10 times.
4. Switch feet and repeat. Benefits: Ankle rotations improve joint mobility and help prevent sprains and strains.

Exercise 5: Adductor Stretch

1. Sit on the floor with your legs extended in front of you.

2. Bend one leg and bring the foot toward the inside of the opposite thigh.
3. Keeping your back straight, lean slowly forward toward the extended leg.
4. Hold the position for 20-30 seconds, then switch sides.
Benefits: This exercise is useful for stretching the adductor muscles, located on the inner thigh, which are important for pelvic stability.

Exercise 6: Hip Flexor Stretch

1. Start in an upright position, then step forward with one leg.
2. Bend both knees at a 90-degree angle, keeping the back knee just above the ground.
3. Push slightly forward until you feel a stretch in the front of the hip of the back leg.

4. Hold for 20-30 seconds, then switch sides. Benefits: This exercise targets the hip flexors, which can stiffen due to sedentary lifestyles or aging, contributing to posture issues and lower back pain.

Exercise 7: Heel Raise

1. Stand with your feet shoulder-width apart.
2. Slowly lift your heels off the ground, coming onto the balls of your feet.
3. Slowly lower your heels back down.
4. Repeat for 10-15 times. Benefits: This simple exercise helps strengthen the calf muscles and improve balance.

Exercise 8: Hamstring Tendon Stretch

1. Sit on a chair and lift one leg, keeping the other planted on the ground.
2. Try to extend the raised leg as much as possible, keeping the heel toward you.
3. Hold the position for 20-30 seconds, then switch legs. Benefits: This exercise is great for stretching the hamstring tendon, helping to improve overall flexibility and reduce the risk of injuries.

Conclusion: Taking care of your legs and knees is crucial for maintaining a good level of physical activity and independence in later life. With these targeted exercises, you can effectively stretch and strengthen the key muscles supporting these areas of the body.

Each of these exercises has the potential to significantly improve your quality of life, especially if you're over 60. Taking the time to perform these exercises can make a big difference in your daily well-being. Always remember to consult your doctor before starting a new exercise routine.

Chapter 8: Extend Your Arms: Stretching for Shoulders and Neck

Introduction

In old age, tension that has accumulated for years in the shoulders and neck can become a bothersome daily problem. Worsening the situation, these issues are often exacerbated by poor posture or a sedentary lifestyle. In this chapter, we'll explore a series of detailed stretching exercises that can help reduce tension in these critical areas.

Exercise 1: Shoulder Rotation

1. Sit or stand with a straight back.
2. Slowly rotate your shoulders forward five times, then backward five times.
3. Repeat for 2-3 sets.

Benefits:
This simple movement can help release accumulated tension in the shoulders and improve circulation in the neck area.

Exercise 2: Lateral Neck Tilt

1. Sit with a straight back.

2. Slowly tilt your head toward one shoulder, trying to touch the shoulder with your ear.
3. Hold for 20-30 seconds, then return to the starting position.
4. Repeat on the other shoulder.

Benefits:
This exercise aims to stretch the lateral muscles of the neck, helps reduce stiffness, and increases flexibility.

Exercise 3: Trapezius Stretch

1. Sit on a chair and grip the seat with one hand.
2. Tilt your head in the opposite direction, extending the neck and shoulder.
3. Hold for 20-30 seconds, then switch sides.

Benefits:
This exercise stretches the trapezius muscles, which are

often involved in tension and neck and shoulder pain.

Exercise 4: Wrist Circulation

1. Extend an arm in front of you with the palm facing down.
2. Using the other hand, grasp the fingers and gently pull them toward you.
3. Hold for 15-20 seconds, then repeat on the other side.

Benefits:
This exercise is particularly useful for those who have issues with arthritis or stiffness in the wrists and hands but is also effective for relieving tension in the shoulders.

Conclusion

Incorporating these exercises into your daily routine can provide significant relief from tension and pain in the neck and shoulders. However, always consult your doctor before starting a new exercise routine, especially if you have pre-existing health issues.

Chapter 9: Flexibility in Hands and Wrists

Many people underestimate the importance of flexibility and strength in the hands and wrists until they start to experience symptoms such as stiffness, pain, or even the inability to perform daily activities like opening a jar. This chapter is dedicated to stretching exercises that help keep hands and wrists agile and healthy, reducing the risk of issues like carpal tunnel syndrome or arthritis.

Exercise 1: Flexor Wrist Stretch

1. Sitting or standing, extend an arm in front of you with the palm facing up.
2. Use the other hand to gently pull the fingers downward, toward the wrist.
3. Hold the position for 15-20 seconds.
4. Repeat for the other side.

Benefits:
This exercise stretches the wrist flexor muscles, often tense due to repetitive movements like typing.

Exercise 2: Extensor Muscle Stretch

1. Extend the arm in front of you with the palm facing down.
2. Use the opposite hand to gently bend the fingers and the wrist downward.

3. Hold for 15-20 seconds.
4. Repeat on the other side.

Benefits:
Improves the flexibility of the wrist and finger extensor muscles, useful in any activity that requires gripping or lifting.

Exercise 3: Wrist Rotation

1. Hold your hands in front of you, wrists together.
2. Slowly rotate the wrists in a circular motion, first in one direction then in the other.
3. Perform 10 rotations per direction.

Benefits:
This exercise helps maintain wrist flexibility and can relieve accumulated tension.

Exercise 4: Finger Stretch

1. Extend one hand in front of you, fingers together.
2. Use the other hand to gently bend the fingers backward, stretching the palm.
3. Hold the position for 10-15 seconds.
4. Repeat for the other hand.

Benefits:
This exercise is excellent for improving finger flexibility and can be particularly useful for those who play musical instruments or type extensively.

Exercise 5: Pinch and Release

1. Sitting comfortably, take a small soft ball or a stress ball.
2. Squeeze the ball in your hand as hard as possible without causing pain.

3. Hold for 5-10 seconds and then release.
4. Repeat for 10 times for each hand.

Benefits:
This exercise strengthens the hand muscles and can improve your ability to grip objects.

Conclusion

Maintaining flexibility in the hands and wrists is crucial not only for daily activities but also to avoid long-term problems like carpal tunnel syndrome and arthritis. The exercises in this chapter are a great starting point for keeping your hands and wrists healthy. As always, if you experience pain during these exercises, consult a medical professional.

Chapter 10: Breathing and Stretching Exercises

Breathing is a fundamental and often overlooked element when it comes to stretching and flexibility. Proper breathing not only improves the oxygenation of muscles but also helps in relaxing them, allowing for a deeper and more effective stretch. This chapter will explore various exercises that incorporate breathing into stretching, improving both your mental and physical well-being.

Exercise 1: Deep Breathing While Stretching the Quadriceps

1. Stand and grasp one foot behind you with one hand.
2. Maintain balance and pull the foot toward your glute.

3. Inhale deeply, trying to relax your thigh muscles.
4. Exhale, gently pull the foot a bit closer to the glute.
5. Hold for 3 breathing cycles. **Benefits:** This exercise stretches the quadriceps and incorporates breathing for a deeper stretch.

Exercise 2: Breathing and Stretching the Back

1. Sit on the ground with crossed legs and bring your hands in front of you.
2. Inhale, elongate the spine.
3. Exhale, bend forward, trying to keep your back straight.
4. Hold the position for 3-5 cycles of deep breathing. **Benefits:** Stretches the spine and relaxes the back muscles.

Exercise 3: Stretching and Breathing for Hip Flexors

1. Get into a lunge position with one foot forward and the other extended behind you.
2. Inhale, align the spine and relax the shoulders.
3. Exhale, gently push the hips forward to stretch the hip flexor of the extended leg.
4. Hold for 3-5 breathing cycles.
Benefits: Stretches the hip flexors and helps improve posture.

Exercise 4: Shoulder Stretch with Controlled Breathing

1. Stand or sit, bring your left arm behind your head and try to reach your right shoulder blade.
2. With your right hand, grasp your left elbow and gently pull it.

3. Inhale, imagine lengthening the arm even more.
4. Exhale, gently pull the elbow a bit closer to the head.
5. Hold for 3-5 breathing cycles, then switch sides. **Benefits:** Stretches shoulder muscles and improves upper body flexibility.

Conclusion

Incorporating breathing into stretching exercises can offer significant benefits for both the mind and body. This mindful practice can improve the effectiveness of your stretching, reduce stress, and increase overall well-being. As always, it's advisable to consult a physician or physiotherapist before starting any new exercise routine, especially if you have pre-existing health issues.

Chapter 11: Preventing Injuries: What to Avoid

Stretching correctly and safely is crucial, especially as you age. Injuries can be both uncomfortable and debilitating, and prevention is much better than cure. In this chapter, we'll provide detailed information on how to avoid common injuries during stretching exercises, including some practical examples.

Common Mistake 1: "Cold" Stretching

What to Avoid: Intensive stretching without adequate warm-up. **Solution:** Example of warm-up - Walk in place or jog lightly for 5-10 minutes.

Common Mistake 2: Holding Tension in Muscles

What to Avoid: Keeping muscles tense during stretching. **Solution:** Example of Relaxation Exercise - Deep breathing while stretching, focusing on relaxing the target muscles.

Common Mistake 3: Excessive Duration of Stretching

What to Avoid: Holding the stretch for an excessively long time, leading to muscle overload. **Solution:** Example of Stretching Time - Hold each stretch position for a maximum of 15-30 seconds, performing 2-3 sets.

Common Mistake 4: Lack of Consistency

What to Avoid: Stretching irregularly or skipping days. **Solution:** Example of Routine - Include 10-15 minutes of stretching at the end of each physical activity, or dedicate specific days of the week to stretching.

Common Mistake 5: Incorrect Technique

What to Avoid: **Performing stretches incorrectly,** increasing the risk of injury. **Solution:** Example of Technique Correction - Watch video tutorials or consult an expert to make sure you are using the correct technique.

Conclusion

Avoiding these common mistakes can make a significant difference in your stretching routine, protect you, and prevent potential injuries and musculoskeletal issues. Before starting any new exercise routine, it is always a good idea to consult a medical professional or physiotherapist, especially if you have pre-existing conditions that could increase your risk of injury.

CHAPTER 12: Daily Stretching Routine

Maintaining bodily flexibility is crucial for avoiding injuries, improving posture, and promoting overall good health, especially as one ages. A daily stretching routine can make the difference between feeling stiff and achy versus feeling agile and vibrant. Below, we offer a detailed action plan, complete with exercises, to incorporate into your daily routine.

1. **Morning Wake-up**: Cat-Cow Stretch Starting Position: On all fours on the floor, hands under shoulders, knees under hips. Execution: Inhale and arch your back towards the ceiling (like a cat) while lowering your head. Exhale, lower your back into a slight concave shape, and

raise your head looking forward. Duration: Repeat 10 times.

2. **After Breakfast**: Standing Side Stretch Starting Position: Standing with feet shoulder-width apart. Execution: Raise one arm above your head and bend laterally towards the opposite side. Hold for 15 seconds, then repeat on the other side. Duration: 2 sets per side.

3. **During a Work Break**: Neck Rotation Starting Position: Sitting comfortably in a chair, back straight. Execution: Slowly tilt your head toward one shoulder, holding for 15 seconds. Repeat for the other shoulder. Then gently rotate your head from one side to the other. Duration: 2 sets in each direction.

4. **Before Lunch**: Ankle Stretch Starting Position: Sitting in a chair. Execution: Lift one foot off the ground and rotate the ankle clockwise for 10 times, then counterclockwise for another 10 times. Switch feet. Duration: 2 sets per foot.
5. **In the Afternoon**: Quadriceps Stretch Starting Position: Standing near a wall or a chair for balance. Execution: Grab your right ankle with your right hand and gently pull your heel towards your glutes. Hold for 20 seconds. Switch legs. Duration: 2 sets per leg.
6. **Before Dinner**: Back Extension Starting Position: Lying face down on the floor, hands placed at the sides of your chest. Execution: Push with your hands to lift your

torso, extending the back. Hold for 15-20 seconds. Duration: Repeat 3 times.

7. **Before Bed**: Deep Leg Stretch Starting Position: Sitting on the floor, legs extended in front of you. Execution: Inhale and extend your arms upwards. Exhale, bend forward trying to touch your feet with your hands. Hold the position for 20-30 seconds. Duration: 3 sets.

Conclusion: This daily stretching routine is designed to engage various muscle groups and can be performed at different times throughout the day. The aim is to keep your body active and flexible, thereby promoting overall well-being. Always remember to listen to your body: if a movement causes pain or discomfort, stop it and, if necessary, consult an expert. Happy stretching!

CHAPTER 13: Stretching for Specific Activities

Not all physical activities have the same impact on the body. Some may put more stress on specific areas than others. That's why it's essential to adapt your stretching routine based on the activity you plan to do. In this chapter, we'll explore how to adapt stretching exercises for three common activities: gardening, golf, and walking.

Gardening

1. **Hand and Thumb Stretch** • **Starting Position**: Standing or sitting, arms extended. • Execution: Grab your thumb with the opposite hand and gently bend it towards your wrist. Hold the position for 15-20 seconds. Switch hands and repeat. • Duration: 2 sets per hand.
2. **Hip Extension** • **Starting Position**: Standing, feet shoulder-width apart. • Execution: Place your hands on your hips and bend backward, pushing your hips forward. Hold for 20 seconds. • Duration: 2 sets.

Golf

1. **Thoracic Rotation** • **Starting Position**: Standing, legs slightly bent, hands on hips. • Execution: Rotate your

torso from one side to the other, keeping your legs stationary. Hold each rotation for 15-20 seconds. • Duration: 2 sets per side.
2. **Wrist and Forearm Stretch** • **Starting Position**: Standing or sitting. • Execution: Extend one arm forward, bend the wrist upward, and use the opposite hand to gently push toward you. Hold for 15-20 seconds and then do the same with the wrist facing downward. • Duration: 2 sets per hand.

Walking

1. **Calf Stretch** • **Starting Position**: Standing, near a wall. • Execution: Place your hands on the wall and step one foot back, keeping both feet flat on the ground. Slightly bend the front knee and push the

back heel toward the floor. Hold for 20-30 seconds. • Duration: 2 sets per leg.

2. **Thigh Stretch (Quadriceps)** • **Starting Position**: Standing, next to a chair or wall for balance. • Execution: Grab the ankle of one leg and gently pull towards your glutes. Hold for 20-30 seconds. • Duration: 2 sets per leg.

Conclusion Each activity has its specific needs in terms of stretching. It's crucial to have a proper warm-up and focus on exercises that prepare the most involved muscle groups. As always, pay close attention to your body during the exercises, and if you feel pain, stop immediately and consult a professional. Happy stretching and enjoyable activity!

CHAPTER 14: Seasonality and Stretching

Adapting your stretching routine to the different seasons of the year is essential to get the most benefit from your exercises. Each season presents unique challenges and opportunities that can influence your stretching practice. Let's take a look.

Winter

1. **Abdominal and Back Stretch**
   - **Starting Position**: Standing or sitting, with a straight back.
   - Execution: Place your hands behind your head and round your back as you exhale. Inhale while returning to the initial position.
   - Duration: 2 sets of 10.

2. **Calf Stretch**
- **Starting Position**: Standing, about a meter away from a wall.
- Execution: Place your hands on the wall and step one foot back, trying to keep the heel on the ground. Hold for 20-30 seconds.
- Duration: 2 sets per leg.

Spring

1. **Dynamic Leg Stretch**
- **Starting Position**: Standing, legs together.
- Execution: Raise one bent leg to chest height and then extend it again. Repeat for the other leg.
- Duration: 2 sets of 10 per leg.

2. **Shoulder Stretch**
- **Starting Position**: Standing or sitting.
- Execution: Bring one arm horizontally across your body. Use the other arm to pull the

horizontal arm toward your chest.
- Duration: 2 sets of 15-20 seconds per arm.

Summer

1. **Hip Flexor Stretch**
   - **Starting Position**: Standing, feet shoulder-width apart.
   - Execution: Take a step forward and bend both knees into a lunge, keeping the front knee over the ankle. Hold for 20 seconds.
   - Duration: 2 sets per leg.
2. **Thoracic Stretch**
   - **Starting Position**: Sitting or standing, arms extended.
   - Execution: Interlace your hands behind your head, slightly bend your elbows, and open your chest by pushing your elbows back. Hold for 20-30 seconds.
   - Duration: 2 sets.

Fall

1. **Quadriceps Stretch**
- **Starting Position**: Standing, next to a chair or wall for support.
- Execution: Grab one ankle and gently pull towards your glutes. Hold for 20-30 seconds.
- Duration: 2 sets per leg.

2. **Ankle Rotations**
- **Starting Position**: Sitting with one leg extended.
- Execution: Rotate the ankle clockwise and then counterclockwise.
- Duration: 2 sets of 10 rotations per ankle.

Conclusion

Each season has its specificities, and adapting your stretching routine accordingly will help you avoid injuries and get the most out of your exercises. Always maintain a mindful attitude and listen to your body during practice.

Chapter 15: Stretching and Nutrition

The importance of nutrition in determining the effectiveness of stretching exercises is often underestimated. Nutrition and stretching are two elements that, when well-coordinated, can improve not only your flexibility but also your overall health. However, poor nutrition can actually reduce the benefits of stretching, and vice versa.

Interaction between Nutrition and Stretching

1. **Energy and Endurance**: Foods high in energy content can help you perform a more effective stretching session.
2. **Recovery**: Proteins and amino acids are essential for muscle repair after intensive stretching.
3. **Inflammation**: Foods rich in antioxidants can reduce inflammation, facilitating better stretching.

Foods to Avoid

1. **Refined Sugars**: Can cause spikes and drops in energy, making it difficult to maintain a consistent stretching routine.
2. **Fatty Foods**: Tend to make the body more rigid and less

responsive to stretching exercises.

Recommended Foods

1. **Fruits and Vegetables**: Provide antioxidants and sustainable energy.
2. **Lean Proteins**: Promote muscle recovery.

Example Exercise: Quadriceps Stretch with Protein-Rich Meal

- **Starting Position**: Standing next to a chair or a support.
- **Execution**: Grab your right ankle with your right hand and pull the ankle towards your glutes. Maintain balance and hold the position.

- **Duration**: 30 seconds per leg.
- **Ideal Time for Exercise**: After a meal rich in lean proteins like chicken breast.

Nutrients that Enhance Stretching

- **Magnesium**: Reduces muscle cramps and improves flexibility.
- **Omega-3**: Reduces inflammation, promoting better performance in stretching.

Example Day Plan

- **Breakfast**: Protein smoothie with fruit and a pinch of chia seeds.
- **Lunch**: Spinach salad with grilled chicken breast.
- **Dinner**: Baked salmon with quinoa and mixed vegetables.

- **Stretching**: 20 minutes of dynamic stretching in the morning and 20 minutes of static stretching in the evening.

Understanding the interaction between nutrition and stretching allows you to optimize both, gaining benefits that go beyond mere flexibility. Use this information to structure a stretching routine and a meal plan that help you reach your health and wellness goals.

Incorporating proper nutrition along with a well-structured stretching routine can yield surprisingly positive results in terms of flexibility, endurance, and overall well-being. A diet lacking in essential nutrients can negatively impact your stretching. Lack of hydration and minerals like magnesium can lead to muscle cramps, while a diet too rich in sugars and fats can cause inflammation, thus reducing the range of motion.

Nutritional Tips to Maximize Stretching

- **Drink at least 2 liters of water a day.**
- **Incorporate foods rich in antioxidants like berries, pomegranates, and leafy green vegetables into your diet.**
- **Consume a lean protein source within 30 minutes after exercise to improve muscle recovery.**

By incorporating these tips and exercises into your daily regimen, you can optimize the results of your stretching exercises and significantly improve your overall health.

Chapter 16: Stretching for Cardiovascular Health

Although stretching is commonly associated with flexibility and muscle relaxation, it also has a positive impact on the cardiovascular system. When we stretch our muscles, we also stimulate blood circulation and contribute to improving heart function.

Impact on Circulation

Stretching helps improve blood circulation throughout the body, which in turn can help lower blood pressure and reduce stress levels on the heart.

Example Exercise: Calf Stretch for Circulation

- **Starting Position**: Stand about a meter away from a wall.
- **Execution**: Place your hands against the wall and take a step forward with one leg, bending the knee. Keep the other leg straight behind you.
- **Duration**: Hold for 30-40 seconds per side.
- **Objective**: This exercise helps stimulate circulation in the legs, which can be particularly beneficial for those who suffer from circulation issues or varicose veins.

Impact on the Heart

Stretching exercises can also help improve heart health by reducing stress and promoting better circulation, which is essential for a healthy heart.

Example Exercise: Chest Stretch for Heart Health

- **Starting Position**: Sit in a chair with a straight back.
- **Execution**: Extend your arms in front of you and then open them so they are perpendicular to your body. Open the chest by squeezing the shoulder blades together.
- **Duration**: Hold for 20-30 seconds.
- **Objective**: This exercise opens the chest and improves circulation, and also helps to reduce stress on the heart.

Tips for Integrating Stretching into Your Cardiovascular Routine

- Combine stretching exercises with cardiovascular activities

like walking, swimming, or cycling for a complete workout.
- Consult a physician before starting any new exercise program, especially if you have pre-existing heart conditions or other health issues.

Benefits of Stretching for Circulation

1. **Improves Blood Circulation**: Regular stretching helps to relax muscles, which in turn allows for better blood flow.
2. **Reduction of Clotting Risk**: Efficient blood flow reduces the risk of clot formation.
3. **Oxygen Supply**: With optimal circulation, organs and tissues receive a greater amount of oxygen.

Impact on the Heart

Stretching can lower blood pressure and help relax the body. This reduces stress on the heart, especially after a tiring or stressful day.

Example Exercise 1: Calf Stretch for Circulation

- **Starting Position**: Stand close to a wall.
- **Execution**: Place your hands on the wall and step one foot back, keeping the heel on the ground and the leg straight. The front leg is bent.
- **Duration**: Hold for 20-30 seconds and then switch sides.

Example Exercise 2: Leg Elevation

- **Starting Position**: Lie on the floor with legs extended and arms at your sides.
- **Execution**: Slowly lift your legs to form a 90-degree angle with the floor, then lower them slowly.
- **Duration**: Repeat 10 times.

Example Exercise 3: Dynamic Arm Stretch

- **Starting Position**: Stand with your legs slightly apart.
- **Execution**: Extend your arms sideways and rotate them in small circles, first forward then backward.
- **Duration**: Rotate for 30 seconds in each direction.

Example Exercise 4: Chest Stretch

- **Starting Position**: Stand or sit.
- **Execution**: Interlace your hands behind your back and lift your arms as high as possible, opening the chest.
- **Duration**: Hold for 20-30 seconds.

By integrating these exercises into your daily routine, you will not only see an improvement in your flexibility but also in your circulation and heart health. It is always recommended to consult a physician or physiotherapist before beginning a new exercise routine, especially if you have pre-existing health conditions.

Chapter 17: The Importance of Rest and Recovery Rest and

recovery are crucial aspects of any exercise routine, and stretching is no exception. It not only helps prevent injuries but also improves sleep quality and speeds up muscle recovery.

The Role of Stretching in Rest and Recovery

1. **Muscle Recovery**: Stretching can help reduce muscle stiffness that often occurs post-exercise.
2. **Sleep Quality**: Light stretching exercises can prepare the body for a deeper, more restorative sleep.
3. **Stress Management**: Stretching can also have a calming effect on the mind, helping to reduce stress and anxiety.

Exercise Example 1: Quadriceps Stretch for Muscle Recovery

- **Starting Position**: Stand next to a wall or a chair for balance.
- **Execution**: Grab your right ankle with your right hand and pull your foot toward your glutes. Keep your back straight.
- **Duration**: Hold for 20-30 seconds, then switch sides.

Exercise Example 2: Spine Stretch for Sleep Quality

- **Starting Position**: Lie down on the floor with your knees bent and feet flat on the floor.
- **Execution**: Rotate your knees to the right while turning your head and shoulders to the left. Extend your arms out to the sides.
- **Duration**: Hold for 20-30 seconds, then switch sides.

Exercise Example 3: Shoulder Stretch for Stress Management

- **Starting Position**: Stand or sit with a straight back.
- **Execution**: Bring your right arm horizontally across your chest. Use your left arm to apply light pressure to your right arm.
- **Duration**: Hold for 20-30 seconds, then switch sides.

Exercise Example 4: Child's Pose for General Relaxation

- **Starting Position**: On all fours on the floor.
- **Execution**: Sit back on your heels and stretch your arms forward on the floor. Lower your chest towards the floor as far as possible.
- **Duration**: Hold for 1-2 minutes.

Benefits of Rest and Recovery

1. **Muscle Repair**: During rest, damaged muscles repair and strengthen, preventing injuries and soreness.
2. **Stress Reduction**: Adequate rest reduces levels of cortisol, a stress hormone, improving mood and overall health.
3. **Improved Cognitive Function**: A good night's sleep can enhance memory, focus, and other cognitive functions.

Relaxing Stretches for Sleep and Recovery

Stretching exercises can help calm the body, relax the muscles, and prepare for a deep, restful sleep.

Exercise Example 1: Spinal Stretch

- **Starting Position**: Lying on the floor, knees bent, feet flat on the floor.
- **Execution**: Bring your knees to your chest and wrap them with your arms, gently rocking from side to side.
- **Duration**: Hold for 1-2 minutes.

Exercise Example 2: Spinal Twist

- **Starting Position**: Lying on the floor, knees bent, feet flat on the floor.
- **Execution**: Keep your shoulders on the ground and rotate your bent knees from one side to the other.
- **Duration**: Hold each twist for 20-30 seconds.

Exercise Example 3: Quadriceps Stretch

- **Starting Position**: Lying on your side, head resting on your arm.
- **Execution**: Grab the ankle of the upper leg and gently pull it towards your glutes.
- **Duration**: Hold for 20-30 seconds per side.

Exercise Example 4: Subscapular Stretch

- **Starting Position**: Sitting or lying down.
- **Execution**: Extend one arm forward and use the other arm to gently push the elbow towards your chest.
- **Duration**: Hold for 20-30 seconds per arm.

Incorporating these stretching exercises into your evening

routine will help relax your body and mind, preparing you for a restful sleep. Always remember to perform each movement slowly and without force, always listening to your body. If you experience pain or too much discomfort, consult a physician or a physiotherapist before starting a new exercise routine.

Chapter 18: Stretching for Mental Health

In the hustle and bustle of modern life, mental health is often neglected. Stress, anxiety, and depression are increasingly common issues. Although stretching may seem like an unusual solution, it's amazing how it can actually contribute to mental well-being.

How Does It Work?

Stretching has the ability to relax both the mind and body simultaneously. When we stretch our muscles, we send signals to the brain that trigger the release of endorphins, the well-being hormones. This can help to reduce symptoms of stress and anxiety.

Targeted Exercises

Example Exercise 1: Neck Stretch

- Starting Position: Sit comfortably in a chair, with a straight back.
- Execution: Slowly tilt your head to one side, trying to touch your ear to your shoulder while keeping the opposite shoulder down.

- Duration: Hold for 15-20 seconds. Repeat on the other side.

Example Exercise 2: Shoulder Stretch

- Starting Position: Stand or sit with relaxed shoulders.
- Execution: Bring your shoulders up towards your ears in an "elevator" motion, then relax them in a "free-fall" motion.
- Duration: 10-15 repetitions.

Example Exercise 3: Forward Bend

- Starting Position: Stand with feet shoulder-width apart.
- Execution: Bend forward at the hips, trying to touch the floor, or if possible, place your hands on the ground.

- Duration: Hold for 20-30 seconds.

Example Exercise 4: Chest Stretch

- Starting Position: Stand or sit.
- Execution: Bring both hands behind your back and, if possible, grasp them together. Lift your arms as high as possible, opening your chest.
- Duration: Hold for 20-30 seconds.

How to Integrate into Daily Routine

To obtain maximum benefits, it's advisable to perform these exercises at least once a day. You can do it in the morning to prepare for a stressful day or in the evening to relax before going to bed.

Precautions

As with all stretching exercises, it's crucial to listen to your body. Never force a movement if you feel pain or discomfort. In cases of severe mental health issues, stretching can be a complement, but not a substitute, for medical and psychotherapeutic treatments.

Mental Strategies During Stretching

Focus: During each exercise, focus on your breathing and physical sensations. This helps you remain present and diverts your attention from anxious thoughts.

Visualization: Imagine that each inhale brings refreshing energy, and each exhale expels stress and tension.

Psychological Mechanisms

1. **Endorphin Release**: Stretching stimulates the production of endorphins, natural painkillers.
2. **Mindfulness**: Focusing on your body and breathing during stretching can have a meditative effect, helping to divert attention from anxious thoughts.
3. **Improved Sleep**: As discussed in previous chapters, stretching can improve sleep quality, a key factor in stress management.

Stretching is not just beneficial for flexibility and physical well-being, but can also be a powerful

tool for your mental health. Implementing these exercises into your daily routine can help you better manage stress and anxiety. As always, if you're new to exercise or have medical concerns, it's advisable to consult a doctor before starting a new exercise routine.

Chapter 19: Water Stretching

Water stretching is an effective way to use the natural resistance of water to improve flexibility and reduce the risk of injury. This form of stretching is ideal for anyone but is particularly useful for the elderly, the unfortunate, and those with mobility issues. Below are some of the main benefits and specific exercises for water stretching.

Benefits of Water Stretching

1. Reduced stress on muscles and joints: Water decreases body weight, offering less stress on the joints during exercise.
2. Increased Resistance: Water offers resistance from all sides, meaning muscles must work a bit harder compared to exercises outside of water.
3. Relaxation and Mental Wellbeing: The sound and feel of water have a calming effect on the nervous system.

Exercise Examples

Calf Stretch

Starting Position: Stand near the edge of the pool.

- Execution: Place the palms of your hands on the edge of the pool and take a step back until you feel a stretch in the calf.
- Duration: Hold for 15-30 seconds. Repeat for the other side.

Adductor Stretch

- Starting Position: Standing with water reaching mid-thigh.
- Execution: Lift one leg to the side and try to stretch it as far as possible while keeping the other leg straight and anchored to the bottom.
- Duration: Hold for 15-30 seconds. Repeat for the other side.

Shoulder Stretch

- Starting Position: In water up to the chest.

- Execution: Extend your arms in front of you, then move them slowly outward, keeping your hands underwater to utilize resistance.
- Duration: Hold the outer position for 10-15 seconds. Repeat.

Back Stretch

- Starting Position: In water up to the waist.
- Execution: Tilt the torso slowly backward, using the arms to balance. You will feel a stretch along the spine and chest.
- Duration: Hold for 15-20 seconds. Repeat.

Water stretching offers an alternative and advantageous option compared to traditional stretching routines. The natural resistance and lower impact on joints make this mode accessible and useful for a wide range of individuals. As always, consulting a physician before starting any new exercise program is advisable.

Further Benefits

1. **Lower Impact on Joints**: The buoyancy of water reduces the effect of gravity, offering a low-impact environment ideal for those with joint issues or injuries.
2. **Greater Resistance**: Water provides natural resistance, helping to strengthen muscles as you stretch them.
3. **Muscle Relaxation**: Water, especially if warm, can help relax tense muscles, making the stretch even more effective.
4. **Improved Circulation**: Water can help stimulate blood

circulation, aiding muscles in obtaining the oxygen they need to function at their best.

More Exercise Examples

... [Due to the character limit, I've truncated the additional exercise examples and concluding paragraphs. You can ask for them separately if needed.]

This translation should give you a comprehensive understanding of water stretching, its benefits, and some example exercises. It is strongly advised to consult a physician or a physical therapist before starting any new exercise routine, especially if you have preexisting medical conditions.

Chapter 20: Stretching and Balance

Why It's Important

Balance is especially crucial in everyday life and useful in preventing falls and injuries. Stretching exercises aimed at improving balance can help enormously.

Example Exercise 1: Tree Yoga Stretch

- **Starting Position:** Standing, feet shoulder-width apart.
- **Execution:** Shift weight onto one foot and rest the other foot on the opposite inner thigh. Raise your arms above your head and hold the position.
- **Duration:** 15-30 seconds per side.

Example Exercise 2: Single Leg Forward Bend

- **Starting Position:** Standing.
- **Execution:** Bend forward on one foot, extending the other foot behind you. Extend your arms in front of you for balance.
- **Duration:** 10-20 seconds per side.

Chapter 21: Clothing and Equipment for Stretching

Wearing comfortable and flexible clothing is essential. Using equipment like resistance bands, foam rollers, or yoga balls can also enrich your stretching routine.

Example Exercise: Stretching with Resistance Band
- **Starting Position:** Sitting.
- **Execution:** Wrap a resistance band around the sole of your foot and hold both ends with your hands. Pull towards you.
- **Duration:** 15-30 seconds per side.

Chapter 22: Stretching and Joint Mobility

Joint health is improved by adequate mobility, which can be facilitated through stretching.

Example Exercise: Ankle Circles
- **Starting Position:** Sitting or standing.

- **Execution:** Rotate the ankle in a circular motion.
- **Duration:** 10 rotations per side.

Chapter 23: Stretching for Active Aging

Stretching can be a vital part of healthy and active aging.

Example Exercise: Arm Stretch with a Chair

- **Starting Position:** Sitting on a chair, feet on the ground.
- **Execution:** Raise one arm and lean to the opposite side.
- **Duration:** 15-30 seconds per side.

Chapter 24: Travel and Stretching

Maintaining a stretching routine while traveling can be challenging but possible with a little planning.

Example Exercise: Stretching on a Plane

- **Starting Position:** Sitting.
- **Execution:** Extend one leg and bend slightly forward from the hip.
- **Duration:** 10-20 seconds per side.

Chapter 25: Community and Stretching

Sharing the practice of stretching with friends and family can make the experience more rewarding and encouraging.

Example Exercise: Partner Stretching

- **Starting Position:** Both standing, facing each other.
- **Execution:** Hold hands, and one person bends forward while the other leans backward.
- **Duration:** 10-20 seconds, then switch roles.

Chapter 26: FAQs - Frequently Asked Questions on Stretching and the Elderly

Why It's Important

Many older people have questions and concerns about integrating stretching into their daily routine. In this chapter, we will address some of the most common questions to help dispel myths and misconceptions.

Question 1: Is it safe to stretch at a certain age?

- **Answer:** Yes, with proper precautions and under the guidance of a healthcare professional or physiotherapist, stretching can be a great addition to an older person's physical activity routine.

Example Exercise: Quadricep Stretch

- **Starting Position:** Standing next to a chair or support.
- **Execution:** Grab one foot and pull it toward the glute, keeping the pelvis straight.
- **Duration:** 15-20 seconds per side.

Question 2: Can stretching exercises help reduce joint pain?

- **Answer:** Yes, stretching can help improve joint mobility and reduce pain if done correctly.

Example Exercise: Calf Stretch
- **Starting Position:** Standing next to a wall.
- **Execution:** Place your hands on the wall and step one foot back. Press the heel down until you feel a stretch in the calf.
- **Duration:** 20-30 seconds per side.

Question 3: How much time should I dedicate to stretching?

- **Answer:** A good starting point could be 15-20 minutes per day, broken into 30-second sessions for each stretching exercise.

Example Exercise: Abdominal Stretch

- **Starting Position:** On the ground, face down.
- **Execution:** Place your hands near your shoulders and push up, rounding your back.
- **Duration:** 15-30 seconds.

Question 4: Can I stretch if I have heart problems?

- **Answer:** Always consult a physician before starting any new exercise routine, especially if you have health concerns like heart diseases.

Question 5: Can stretching exercises be done at home?

- **Answer:** Absolutely, yes. Many stretching routines can be comfortably done at home with very little equipment.

Example Exercise: Back Stretch

- **Starting Position:** Sitting on a chair.
- **Execution:** Lean forward, trying to touch the floor with your hands.
- **Duration:** 15-30 seconds.

Remember to always consult a doctor or physiotherapist before starting a new exercise routine, especially if you're elderly or have medical concerns.

Chapter 27: Conclusion and Action Plan

The Journey So Far We have explored the world of stretching in detail, from its mental and physical health benefits to specific exercises targeting various body parts and age groups. Stretching is a versatile and inclusive practice that can improve anyone's quality of life, regardless of age or fitness level.

Example of a Daily Routine
To implement a stretching routine into your daily life, here's a detailed action plan:

1. **Morning Stretching**
   - Quad Stretch: 20 seconds per leg
   - Shoulder Stretch: 15 seconds per shoulder
2. **Afternoon Stretch**
   - Wrist Stretch: 15 seconds per wrist
   - Neck Stretch: 20 seconds per side

3. **Evening Stretch**
   - Abdominal Stretch: 30 seconds
   - Calf Stretch: 20 seconds per leg
4. **Pre-Sleep Stretch**
   - Deep Breathing Exercises: 5 inhale/exhale cycles
5. **As-Needed Stretching**
   - Take breaks to perform targeted stretches, especially if you have a sedentary job, like back or hand stretches.

Practical Tips

- **Consistency**: The key to reaping the benefits of stretching is being consistent. Even 5 minutes a day can make a difference.
- **Personalization**: Tailor the exercises to your needs. If you have back problems, focus on

stretches that relieve tension in that area.

- **Medical Consultation**: Always consult a doctor or physiotherapist before starting any new exercise routine, especially if you have preexisting health issues.

Your Commitment
By applying these tips and exercises, you'll have the necessary tools to begin a healthier, more active life. From here on, success depends on your dedication in making stretching an integral part of your daily routine. Remember, your health is an investment, not an expense. With that, we wish you a peaceful and rewarding journey into the world of stretching.

In conclusion, it's crucial to emphasize the importance of stretching in daily life. Although often underestimated, stretching not only helps maintain good flexibility and prevent injuries, but it can also improve posture, reduce pain and stress, and boost circulation.

Summary of Benefits:

1. **Flexibility**: Greater flexibility allows you to perform daily activities more easily and with less pain.
2. **Injury Prevention**: A good stretching routine can help prevent injuries, particularly during physical activities.
3. **Improved Posture**: Regular stretching can help correct and maintain good posture.

4. **Relaxation**: Many stretching exercises promote relaxation and help in stress management.

Action Plan:

1. **Assessment**: Before you start, evaluate your level of flexibility to better focus your efforts. *Example Exercise: Forearm Flexibility Test*
   - Starting Position: Arms extended forward.
   - Execution: Try to touch your thumb with your pinky. If you can't, it indicates reduced forearm flexibility.
2. **Establish a Routine**: Choose a time of day to dedicate 15-20 minutes to stretching. *Example Exercise: Morning Shoulder Stretch*
   - Starting Position: Standing or sitting.

- Execution: Raise your arms and interlock your hands, then push your hands forward until you feel a stretch in the shoulders.
- Duration: 20-30 seconds.

3. **Vary the Exercises**: Make sure to change the exercises to avoid monotony and to work on different parts of the body. *Example Exercise: Ankle Rotations*
    - Starting Position: Sitting on a chair.
    - Execution: Lift one foot and rotate the ankle clockwise, then counter-clockwise.
    - Duration: 10 rotations per direction.
4. **Monitor Progress**: Record your routine and progress. This will help you stay motivated

and see areas where you can improve.

5. **Advice**: Listen to your body. If you feel pain (not to be confused with slight discomfort), stop and seek medical advice. Also, make sure to stretch with warmed-up muscles. You can take a short walk or perform some dynamic movements before starting.

Finally, make stretching an integral part of your life. It can be a time for yourself to relax and take care of your body. With consistency and dedication, you'll reap the benefits of greater flexibility and overall well-being.

Epilogue

Remember, stretching is not just an activity; it's a long-term investment in your well-being. And like any investment, the benefits will grow over time. So, grab the mat, stretch your arms, and take the first step on this journey toward a better you.

No matter where you are in life, there's always room to improve, to stretch a bit further, and to reach a new level of well-being. And this book, we hope, has provided you with the tools to do so.

Thank you for reading and happy stretching to all!

Chase Williams

Made in the USA
Coppell, TX
21 October 2023